MORE!

AWESOME JOKES

VOL 2

EVERY

YEAR OLD
SHOULD
KNOW!

MW00914738

Design: Fanni Williams / thehappycolourstudio.com
Icons made by: Freepik from www.flaticon.com

www.matwaugh.co.uk

Produced by Big Red Button Books,
a division of Say So Media Ltd.

ISBN: 978-1-912883-12-7

Published: July 2019

A note for parents and readers from the USA: I'm British. I can't help it. I'm a bloke
who goes on holiday for a fortnight, never uses a washroom and comes home knackered.
I don't have a Scooby-Doo who the Red Sox are, or what I should do with a doohickey. I've
taken out any jokes about the Queen (sorry, Ma'am), but you may still find a few that
aren't your cup of tea. The rest? Hopefully they're the bee's knees!

MORE!

MORE!

MORE!

AWESOME JOKES

VOL 2

EVERY 8 YEAR OLD SHOULD KNOW!

MAT WAUGH

ILLUSTRATIONS BY INDREK SILVER EINBERG

Hey – you're back!

I have the memory of a goldfish, but I'm sure we've met somewhere before... did you read the first book of Awesome Jokes? You did?

Wow, haven't you grown!

Doesn't it drive you crackers when adults say that? When you're dragged along to see Great Aunt Nelly and she leans down with her whiffy coffee breath and gives you a hug? Yuck.

There's none of that nonsense here – just a bulging, squirming sack of jokes that I've been raising in my back garden. Expect cheeky ones, shrieky ones, and even a few sneaky ones to make you think!

Ready? It's time to pull out a wriggler, let it go and see who laughs!

This sign means the joke is a super-tough nut to crack. Do you get them all?

PS Got your own tip-top joke? Get it on the **World Map of Awesome Jokes**! *See page 89.*

↓ Laughs start here ↓

What does a cobbler always keep in his toolbelt?
A hammer and some toe nails!

How do you put up heavy shelves?
With a handful of walnuts!

What do you throw for a dog in the dark?
A candle stick!

How do trifles get into the swimming pool?
With a jellyflop!

Which pet needs cleaning but not feeding?
A carpet!

How do you know when a snake is getting angry?
When it throws a hissy fit!

 Have you seen my new phone?
It's great for music, but
terrible at making calls.
It's a xylophone!

Every day my Dad gives me a ball. "GET
DRESSED, IT'S TIME FOR SCHOOL!" he bawls.

Why is it easy to slice a chocolate log?

Because it's a piece of cake!

If you call your first three pet gorillas
April, May and June, what name should you
give to the next one?
Perhaps you should call it a day!

Did you hear about the stickmen who tried wrestling?
It turned into a game of snap!

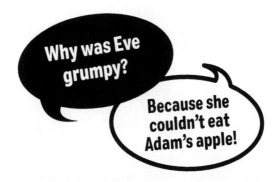

Why was Eve grumpy?

Because she couldn't eat Adam's apple!

What did one skeleton say to the other?
Why are you dressed up like a dog's dinner?

Who's there?
Cash!
Cash who?
Cashew nuts for sale, wanna buy some?

Why do weightlifters make great parents?
They don't like to put you down!

How are you getting on so far? Is it all making sense? Here's another one for you:

What do you call a silly sentence?
An idiom!

That's not only the world's unfunniest joke, it's the secret to lots of funnies in this book. An idiom is a phrase or sentence that doesn't mean what it says. Work them out – or look them up – and you've got the joke!

I bet you already know hundreds of idioms. Some are **a piece of cake** (easy peasy), others are a bit more **thorny** (tricky)!

If they **drive you crazy** or some jokes in this book **have you stumped**, then **hang in there** – or maybe **sleep on it** and **pick someone's brains** tomorrow!

Why do birds often cheat in mazes?
Because they can always take the easy way out!

What tool do criminal birds use?
A crowbar!

How can you get fit without leaving the house?
Run a bath!

Who's the kindest person in a circus?
A trapeze artist, because they'll bend over backwards to help!

What is Cyclops' family motto?
Always Keep An Eye Out for Children!

**Why did the boy train to be a
human cannonball?**
He'd always dreamed of
being a big shot!

**What did the girl say when she tried out
the new living room couch?**
Sofa, so good!

Who's there?
Ammonia.
Ammonia who?
**Ammonia girl that can't
reach the doorbell!**

Do you like my new doorbell?
Not really.
Why not?
I just can't put my finger on it!

What did King Kong do when they ran out of strawberry milkshake?
He went bananas!

What's the only time you get sent home for doing well in a spelling test?
When you get **diarrhoea!** *(or is it diarrhea? Either way, you don't want to get it!)*

How do boring opera singers warm up?
"Blah, blah, blah, blah, blah!"

Why do farmers know so much?

They're experts in their field!

WARNING: BEAN JOKES AHEAD!

What do you call a vegetable on a diet?
Broad-been!

What do you call a retired athlete?
Runner-been!

What do you call a sack with a hole in it?
Been-bag!

What do you call a broken broomstick?
Been-pole!

What do you call a ripe banana?
Green-been!

What's a sheep's favourite motto?
All's wool that ends wool!

How do you stay alive in the desert?
Thirst things first!

What do you call an old people's home for farmers?
Past-ure Best!

What do lumberjacks wear in winter?
A fir hat!

What's the best cure for a twitchy eye?

Forty winks!

What did Goldilocks say when she walked into the house?
Ooh, I love the soft fur-nishings!

Why did the bee cry when he couldn't get to the party?
Because he missed the buzz!

Why should you never make big plans with a hot air balloon pilot?
Because they'll always bring you back down to earth with a bump!

Who's there?
Amanda!
Amanda who?
Amanda fix your washing machine!

 Why did the man buy the bird that sounded like a cat?
Because it was going cheep-purr!

My uncle has five nipples. He has to buy special t-shirts, but they fit like a glove.

Why do glue factories have security guards?
In case there's a stick up!

Did you enjoy that film about hurricanes?
Oh yes! It blew me away.

Knock Knock! --- Who's there?
Hive!
Hive who?
Hive forgotten my key, now let me in!

What do you call a scary dog?
PETrifying!

What is the beekeeper's motto?

Bee prepared!

What's the loudest sound at a birdwatchers' picnic?
Swallows!

What do you call cows in the wrong field?
Miss-herd!

Why should idiots keep hairdryers away from their ears?
Because they'll blow their mind!

What do you call a theme park for kittens?
A mews-ment park!

Why are chickens so rude?

Because they're all fowl-mouthed!

What do you call a cow for sale?
Afford-a-bull!

What do you call a cow with plastic horns?
Like-a-bull!

Who are the most patient people in the world?
Queue-waitees!

...and who are the fastest?
Russians!

What did one romantic shoelace say to another?
Why don't we tie the knot?

... and how did it reply?
Sure – I was at a loose end anyway!

Why did the cookie confess?
It crumbled under pressure!

What's a crab's favourite music?
Rock!

How did Robin Hood put his weapons away?
With a bow tie!

Why are tall teachers the worst?
They're always breathing down your neck!

What do you call a sleepy baker?
A few sandwiches short of a picnic!

What do you call a silly builder?
A few bricks short of a load!

Why are caterpillars so cheerful?
Because every day they turn over a new leaf!

Why did the balloon man lose his job?
He let himself go!

What do you call a man with a football as a hat?
Level-headed!

Why did the boy write the answers on his bedding?
His teacher told him to make a cheat sheet!

What's a French dog's favourite ice cream?
Gar-lick!

**What do you call a heavenly spirit
eating ice cream?**
Angel-lick!

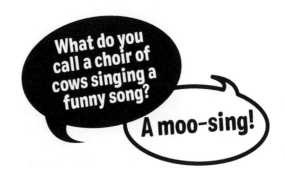

What do you call a choir of cows singing a funny song?

A moo-sing!

**What's the fastest milk
on the shelf?**
Past-your-eyesed!

**What do you call it when you spill glue on
your Grandad's floor?**
A sticky situation!

How do you make a bandstand?
Take away their chairs!

What do you call a sheep that serves drinks?
A baa-maid!

Doctor, Doctor! I feel like an old-fashioned toy!
Is this a wind up?

Why did the stuck-up skeleton not go to the party?
He said he wouldn't be seen dead on the dancefloor!

How do you know when your new teacher is a vegetarian?
When you've been taught by herbivore!

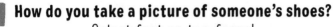

How do you take a picture of someone's shoes?
Select foot or-toe-focus!

Why did the girl visit the fancy dress shop?
Because she'd heard that's where the bigwigs hang out!

Why can't greyhounds concentrate in meetings?
By the time you ask them a question they're miles away!

LOVE CHICKEN JOKES? LET'S CRACK O

What do you call a chicken with dumbbells?
Strengthen!

What do you call a chicken with a tape measure?
Lengthen!

What do you call a chicken with great dance moves?
Smoothen!

What do you call someone who keeps chickens as pets?
Lichen! (Like hen! Geddit?)

What do you call a small speed bump?
A baby bump!

How do strict bees punish their children?
With bees whacks!

What do you call hairy rich men?
Billion-hairs!

Why did the prisoner feel dizzy?
He was in a carou-cell!

How fast does a joker drive?
100 smiles per hour!

Why don't dogs like frying pans?
Because they're non-stick!

How does an elephant learn tennis?
He plays it by ear!

How do you make someone sick on their birthday?
Give them the mumps!

How do you sign in to your mum's computer?
Use 'er name!

How does a musician tell a conductor that she's ill?
She sends a sick note!

Knock Knock!

Who's there?
Angelina!
Angelina who?
Angel in a spot of bother, my wings have fallen off!

**My Dad can't drive straight.
That's why his car has so many acci-dents!**

Knock Knock!

Who's there?
Juliette!
Juliette who?
Juliette my lunch and now I'm starving!

 **I can't tell if I'm standing up or lying down!**
Here, strap this to your arm.
What is it?
A lie detector.

What do crabs have on their birthday?

A shell-ebration!

...and what do you call a crab that won't lend you his toys?
Very shellfish!

What do you get if an asteroid lands on your apartment?
Flatmates!

Where does a shark buy her lunch?
At Subwaves!

Did you hear about the man who was sent to jail for stealing luggage?
It was just a briefcase!

What musical instrument does the Yeti play?
Hair guitar!

What do you call a book of dinosaur names?
The-saurus!

Where do clever fish work?
In a think tank!

... and who's in charge?
The tank commander!

Where do ants go skiing?
The ant-arctic!

What do you call a clean dinosaur?
Ex-stinked!

How do decorators go to the toilet?
They paper over the cracks!

Why are twins so bad at pottery?
Because every time they try, it goes pair-shaped!

Which dog makes the quickest ice cream?

A whippet!

What kind of holidays do referees take?
A whistle stop tour!

Why should you never share a picnic with a boxer?
Because he'll always pack a punch!

Why did the dog have a nightmare?
He dreamed he was sleeping ruff!

Why did the dolphin order too much stuff online?
It double-clicked!

A RING JOKE FOR EVERY FINGER!

What do you call a ring that's never where you left it?
Wander-ring!

What do you call a ring that tries to trick you?
A red herr-ring!

What do you call a black and white ring that you get by nagging your mum?
Pander-ring!

What do you call a ring that looks at you funny?
Glare-ring!

What do you call the loudest ring in town?
Blare-ring!

Knock Knock!

Who's there?
Waddle!
Waddle who?
Waddle you do when I'm gone?

5 WEE JOKES FOR CHILDREN ONLY!

[Grown-ups won't like these ones!]

What do you call a wee when you're sitting down?
Bumpee!

What do you call a wee on a trampoline?
Jumpee!

What do you call a wee on a wobbly toilet?
Tippee!

What do you call a wee in the snow?
Nippee!

What do you call a wee by a crocodile-infested lake?
Snappee!

What do you call the maths lesson after lunch?
Calcu-later!

...and what do you call a broken-down car?
Travel-later!

What time do domino players arrive?
On the dot!

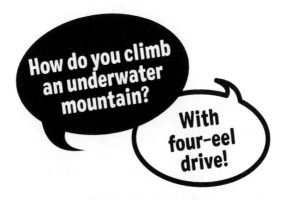

How do you climb an underwater mountain?

With four-eel drive!

How does a duck find out what he's getting for his birthday?
He takes a sneak beak!

 **I've been standing on these scales for ten minutes. What's wrong with me?**
The weight is over. You're obese!

What did one shoe-maker say to the other?
You're my sole mate!

What do you call an elephant with nothing important to say?
Irrelephant!

What makes a robot so attractive?
Magnet-eyes!

Which shower leaves fingerprints on your sofa?
A baby shower!

Why did the librarian go to prison?
He got caught in a book case!

What do you call a man who thinks the fog will clear soon?
An optimist!

Surely Shelley should shred silk shawls?

TONGUE TWISTER

How did the girl find her way into the secret garden?
She made an entry in her diary!

Waiter, Waiter!

This Surf and Turf is a disgrace – there's no meat in it! What do you have to say?
I'd call it a simple miss-steak, sir.

How do llamas get a divorce?
They just spit up!

What's the wrong way to hold your pen?
Write side up!

What's a POP star's favourite school subject?
Fizz-ics!

What do you get if you sit on your granny's sewing box?
Pins and needles!

What is a dog's favourite way to get exercise?
The backstroke!

When is the most dangerous time to wear a suit of armour?

Knight-fall!

Why is this joke like a queue of terrible boxers?
Because of the awful punchline.

Who's there?
Wendy!
Wendy who?
Wendy clock strikes six, I'll be home for tea!

What do you call a man in armour, whistling in a storm?

A knight-in-gale!

How do you describe a comedian who wears his underwear backwards?
Flippant!

My dog was sick on the carpet.
Mum wanted to clear it up before we had dinner, but Dad put his foot down.

Where do they make you leave your lance at the door?

At a knight-club!

Teacher: If it takes you 3 minutes to eat 1 sweet and you have 20 sweets, how long will it take you to eat the whole bag?
Me: That's just a question of time, Miss!

My granddad ran a kebab shop, but after he died I sold the business. He's probably turning in his grave now!

SIX SHARP HEDGEHOG JOKES!

What do you call a chilly hedgehog?
Freezing point!

What do you call hedgehog twins?
Match point!

What do you call a hedgehog at a red light?
Stopping point!

What do you call a hedgehog that won't come back?
Point of no return!

What do you call a hedgehog with superglue?
Sticking point!

What do you call a sad hedgehog in a ditch?
A low point!

My uncle started a hot air balloon company, but he couldn't get it off the ground.

DOCTOR, DOCTOR! ➕

My eyesight is getting worse every day!
Hmm. Can you see the hole in this needle?
Yes!
Then I'm sure you'll pull through.

What do you call a bird that sits on your wrist?
A bang-gull!

Which animal nibbles beards?
A chinchilla!

Waiter, Waiter!

I asked for medium rare. This steak is well done.
Excellent. I'll tell the chef how happy you are, sir!

You must be joking!

Humph... this section makes me grumpy. Since Book 1, eight year olds from around the world have been sending me their jokes. I wouldn't mind because I love getting emails. But the problem is... THEY'RE FUNNY.

This is not how it's supposed to work. Grown-ups know best. Grown-ups *are* the best. Just leave the funnies to me, OK? 😠

RORY FROM YORK, UK

What's the difference between a buffalo and a bison?

You can't wash your hands in a buffalo!

HENRY FROM CINCINNATI, USA

How many paws does a cat have?

Two front paws, two back paws and two grandpas!

What dog is brown and has mustard on its head?

A sausage dog!

Why did the man put his alarm clock on the train?

Which country eats the most food?

So he could time travel!

Hungary!

Who stole the soap?

A robber duckie!

Excuse me, I would like to get a kitten for my son. Have you got any going cheap?

Of course not, they all go meow!

What happened to the zombie that got stung by a bee?

He turned into a zomBEE!

Knock, Knock!
Who's there?
Axed.
Axed who?
You axed for it, this is another Knock, Knock! joke!

What is the difference between a well dressed man and a tired dog?

One is in a suit, the other just pants!

Do you have a great joke? Get it on the **World Map of Awesome Jokes** – see page 89!

Knock Knock!

Who's there?
Quarter!
Quarter who?
Quarter finger in the door, open up quick!

Why do cowboys make the best sketch artists?
They're always quick on the draw!

How do you describe a marching band of bees?
Humdrum!

What do you call a grape as big as an apple?
Beyond a choke!

Waiter, Waiter!

Will this pudding help me lose weight?
Oh yes, sir, it's almost inedible!

Why is it easy to fool a teddy bear?
Because they're a soft touch!

What do you call a lamb on second-hand rollerblades?
A sheepskate!

What does a shepherd put his carrot sticks in?
Sheep dip!

How does a sheep surf the internet?
Using the scroll baa!

How do people with dry lips eat Chinese food?
With a pair of chapsticks!

Why was the treasure hunter excited when he found the pirates' playing cards?
Because everyone knows that pirates keep their cards close to their chest!

How does a clam read at night?
With a clamp!

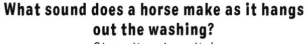

What sound does a horse make as it hangs out the washing?
Clop clip, clop clip!

Why is it pointless to steal a clock?
Because everyone knows you have to put them back
in the autumn! (or fall!)

 **Is it normal to carry a
mackerel in my pocket?**
Absolutely. Everyone feels a fish
out of water from time to time.

When do ducks go on holiday?
Beak season!

**What did one cow say to the other when they
met over a hedge?**
I'm not sure who you are, but your face rings a bell!

BEWARE TERRIBLE TEACHERS!

What do you call a bad ballet teacher?
Miss Steps!

What do you call a bad archery instructor?
Miss Fire!

What do you call a bad baseball coach?
Miss Hits!

What do you call a teacher who gets the class lost on school trips?
Miss Led!

What do you call a choir teacher who's never there?
Miss Sing!

What do you call a judge who needs the toilet?
Court short!

 **My twins aren't good at sharing. Could they take anything to make things better?**
Turns?

Did you hear about the old man who mistook the cleaning cupboard for the bathroom?
He kicked the bucket.

How do mathematicians settle an argument over the bill?
They draw a line under it!

 **My son put washing up liquid in my drink!**
How do you feel now? Sick? Angry?
Angry? I'm foaming at the mouth!

Which are the noisiest animals at a funeral?
The wails!

How do you fit an elephant into your freezer?
Simple – take the moose out, put the elephant in!

What do you call that terrible feeling when you know you've got your sums wrong?
The aftermath!

How does a hen buy online?

Point and cluck!

How does an elephant get to the top of a cherry tree?
He sits on the stone and waits until it grows!

Have you joined the Punctuation Club?
I haven't heard of that. Is it fun?
Oh yes. They're very friendly to newcomers.
[Newcomers.. New commas.. get it now?]

What do bakers fit to the car roof when they go on holiday?
A toast rack!

...and did you hear about the bakers who had a child?
They raised a toast!

 **I can hear ringing in my ears, like a telephone. What should I do?**
Perhaps you should answer it? It's your call.

What does a boxer serve for lunch?
A snack in the face!

Why don't musicians like journalists?
They're always taking notes!

What's a ghost's favourite drink?

Booze!

Why were Tweedledum and Tweedledee angry?
Because Alice threw the looking-glass!

What do you call a bald man in a grizzly costume?
Bear-headed!

What's a sheep's favourite feeling?
Shear delight!

**The oldest postman in the world died last week.
He had a great send off!**

How do you give a polar bear his dinner?

Sealed, with a kiss!

Waiter, Waiter!

Will we have to wait long for a table?
I doubt it, sir. Most people leave after the first course!

What do baby pandas have in their swimming pool?
Bamboo chutes!

What's the worst cruise ship in the world?
A bin liner!

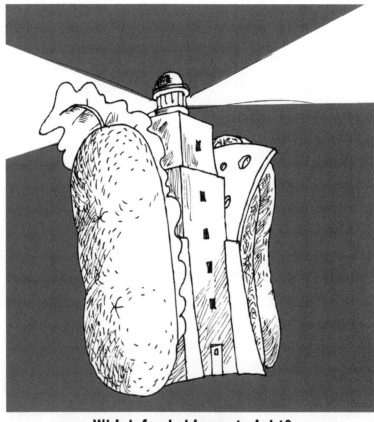

Which food shines at night?
A beacon sandwich!

Why do racing drivers go round in circles?
Because one good turn deserves another!

 **Which percussion instrument always goes missing?**
The steal drums!

I've built some steps to get over my garden wall! How do they look?
Very stile-ish!

When are you going to fill that gap in your herb garden?
As soon as I have the thyme!

Where's the best place to make bread?
In a high rise building!

What is a potato farmer's favourite ice cream?

Chocolate chip!

THIS IS THE TRICKIEST SET OF JOKES...

What do you call a boy who's stuck in a river?
Adam!

What do you call a boy who can make honey with his feet?
Toby!

Which boy lets others try first?
Hugo!

What do you call a boy with a head for heights?
Tyler!

What do you call his girlfriend?
Ruth!

What do you call a boy inside an envelope?
Ismail!

What do you call a boy with everything you need?
Kit!

What do you call a girl dressed in bubblewrap?
Poppy!

What do you call a girl who goes DONG every time she bends over?
Isabelle!

What do you call a girl who sells expensive honey?
Phoebe!

What do you call a girl who knows how to spell *salmon* **and** *chalk***?**
Elsie! (use the pic to work this tricky one out!)

What do you call a girl on crutches?
Lena...!

What happens if you get food on the doorknob?
Your Dad flies off the handle!

Why was the short girl kicked off the basketball team?
Because she couldn't catch UP!

What do you call a man who drops the coffin?
A blundertaker!

What's the best place to hide treasure in a coffee shop?
Under grounds!

My wife climbed up to the attic last week and I haven't seen her since!
Don't worry, I expect she's just coming down with something.

Why did the teacher wear a pencil sharpener as a hat?
He wanted to make a point!

Did you hear about the baby who screamed so loud his neighbours dropped dead?
They say it was a killer wail!

What do you call a glue spillage in a shoe shop?
Sole-destroying!

 **Why do trombone players make the best foot doctors?**
They'll blow your socks off!

I've just bought a table that tells me what I'm reading next.
Wow, what's it called?
A table of contents!

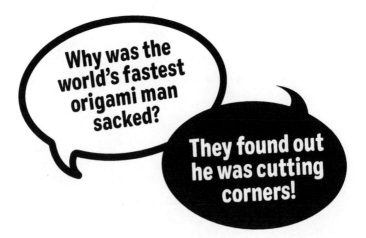

Why was the world's fastest origami man sacked?

They found out he was cutting corners!

Did you hear about the tea farmer who fell into the lake?
He strained his back!

What do you call identical llamas?
Spitting images!

**How do you get out of an argument
with a polar bear?**
Just hang on – eventually they'll go with the floe!

How did the curtains end their argument?
They agreed to meet halfway!

I can't look left or right!
Don't worry, I'm sure you have a bright future ahead of you!

Why are mountaineers such poor marathon runners?
Because they always have a crampon!

How do you know an elephant's name just by looking at its bottom?
Search for a tell-tail sign!

Did you hear about the dog who came home with an alien in its mouth?
Really? That sounds a bit far-fetched!

Why are tailors such great story tellers?
They'll soon have you in stitches!

Why are tunnel diggers the quickest to understand a problem?
Because they're always first to see the light!

What do you call a pig hiding in a hedge?
A hambush!

Every time I sneeze, my Dad sprays me with kitchen cleaner. He's treating me like dirt!

That's nothing. My football coach is the same. Every week, he wipes the floor with me!

What's a vampire's favourite flower?
Deadly nightshade!

How do police handle luggage theft?

On a case by case basis!

How do you make an hour feel like a minute?
Buy a *second hand* clock!

How do you lift a thousand forks?
With a forklift truck, of course!

Waiter, Waiter!

I've just cut my lip on your strawberry tart!
The menu did say it was glazed, sir!

What's the best way to catch a dog that steals your food?
With a steak-out!

Why do bees with curly hair fly faster?

Because they're frizz-bees!

Why do astronauts travel so fast?
Because they always speed UP!

Waiter, Waiter!

This fish hasn't been cured properly!
I'm sorry sir, I didn't even know it was ill!

What do you give a bee with chilly legs?
A bee-knee hat!

DOCTOR, DOCTOR!

My bottom looks like the Ace of Hearts! Can you help me?
Let me have a look. I'm sure I can deal with it.

My grandad often takes strolls up a mountain –
but he doesn't always bring them home again!

What do chickens do on holiday?

Egg-scream sports!

What do you call an envelope that's held up in traffic?
Stationery!

What do you call a caveman who hunts after dark?
A night clubber!

Why was the boy in floods of tears after meeting his girlfriend?
Because they had a stormy relationship!

...and why did he have burn marks on his shoes?
Because they'd had a blazing row!

They're back together now, so why do they feel seasick?
Because they'd been through a rough patch!

 **Is it true that you charge your patients every time they ask a question?**
I'm sorry, could you say that again?

Why should you never give a giraffe a lift on a rainy day?
Because you'll never close the sunroof!

HERE'S 10 OF THE BEST BULL JOKES...

What do you call cowpats all over your bedroom floor?
Indescribe-a-bull!

What do you call a cow that's great at chess?
Unpredict-a-bull!

What do you call a cow that's great at hide and seek?
Undiscover-a-bull!

What do you call a million pound cow?
Unafford-a-bull!

What do you call a cow in high heels and earrings?
Fashion-a-bull!

What do you call a cow you invited to your birthday party?
Regrett-a-bull!

What do you call a cow that won't drink enough water?
Un-full-fill-a-bull!

What do you call a cow that lands on your house?
Impression-a-bull!

What do you call a cow arrested by police?
Question-a-bull!

... and what do you call a cow that refuses to tell them anything?
Unquestion-a-bull!

Waiter, waiter! This meat is very tough and you've forgotten the fries!
I'm sorry sir, the restaurant is next door –
this is a shoe shop.

 **DOCTOR, DOCTOR!**

I feel like a pack of cards! Do you have any advice for me?
You bet!

What do you call four pigs on a road trip?
Four squeal drive!

Why do jigsaws make terrible soldiers?
Because they always go to pieces!

What do you call a priest who performs pirouettes?
Just praying around!

How does a weatherman lock his front door?
With a lightning bolt!

How does a racing driver become a chauffeur?
Change gear!

What did the daddy bat say to the baby bat?
Don't worry, you'll soon get the hang of it!

Why are Eskimos great at parties?
Because they know how to break the ice!

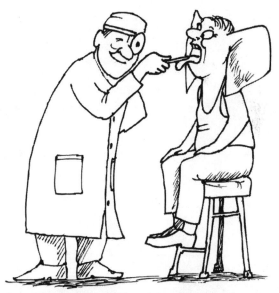

**Doctor, Doctor! I've heard there's elephant
flu around and I think I've caught it!**
You look absolutely fine – I've never heard such
mumbo-jumbo!

Did you hear about the special agent owls?
They hoot to kill!!

How do you order shoes online?
Just click your heels!

Where do you go to get the best banana smoothies?

Monkey bars!

I'm having trouble with my figure!
Then take this abacus.
Will it help me lose weight?
Oh yes, you can count on it!

Why couldn't the electrician fit a new floor light?
He screwed up!

Waiter, Waiter!

This chicken is undercooked!
It looks OK to me, sir, what makes you so sure?
It's just a gut feeling!

Why did the surfer take his keyboard back to the shop?
The C was missing!

DOCTOR, DOCTOR!

There's enough wax in my ears to make candles!
How do you feel?
Light-headed!

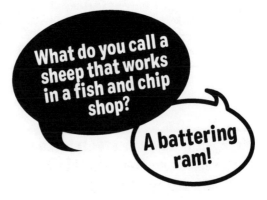

What do you call a sheep that works in a fish and chip shop?

A battering ram!

What is Pinocchio's favourite food?
Woodchips!

We went to a little beach last summer, but my sister was stung as soon as she sat down. She's a bay bee sitter!

Where's the best place to buy underwear?
At the bottom end of the market!

How do you make a sandcastle out of ice cream?
Lick it into shape!

Why do clowns never retire?
Because nobody can fill their boots!

Which bird tells the funniest stories?
A wag-tale!

What do you call a man who drowns cornflakes?
A cereal killer!

Why was the butcher nearly late for lunch?

He was cutting it fine!

How did the scarecrow get the waiter's attention?
He snapped his fingers!

Which animal won't let you in without a ticket?
A dormouse!

Where did cavemen sleep?
On bedrock!

Which member of the orchestra gets to rehearsal first?
The bassoonist!

How does a kindergarten keep the lights on?
With blackcurrant!

This party is great! But what happened to your plan for a trampolining elephant?
It fell through!

My dentist is going to give me chocolate for my fillings.
Are you sure?
Yes! He said he'll be sure to treat me well!

Bad news: parents have been allowing their dogs to poo on the playing field.
Good news: the headmaster has promised to stamp down on it!

Did you hear about the vampire who kept crashing into church bells?
It was a dingbat!

Which animals love card games?
The lambs, because they love to gambol!

How do you make a scarf for a giraffe?
Sew far, sew good!

What do rubbish collectors wear on rainy days?
Waste coats!

Now it's your turn!

Writing jokes is simple, isn't it? You just think of something funny!

But that's where it gets a bit tricky, because people laugh at different things depending on their background, mood, nationality and lots of other things you can't control. If you've ever said the most hilarious thing possible and people look like you've just made a horrible smell, then you know what I mean!

But don't worry – if you make up a joke that gets *most* people chuckling, you've got a good one.

So then: would you like the chance to show the world how hilarious you are? Now's your chance!

If you already have a humdinger, then read on. But if you fancy writing your own, and you like drawing too, then get your thinking cap on and your pencils ready, and turn to page 90!

I know a great joke!

If you're sitting on a zinger, there are two possibilities:

1 – your bottom is a bit itchy
2 – you already have a brilliant, clever and super funny joke.

If it's number 1, I recommend that you see a doctor, pronto.

If it's number 2, then send your joke to me and I'll put it on my **World Map of Awesome Jokes**!

Head over to the map now to discover silly jokes, clever jokes and weird jokes. Some jokes rhyme, some are a crime, but they're all sent in by children like you!

Could you be the first on the map from your town?

et a grown-up to send in your joke:
www.matwaugh.co.uk/jokemap

Jokers wanted!

Could you write and illustrate your own joke?

There are lots of different types of jokes. Many jokes use *surprise*. Think about this classic (not one of mine!):

> **What's brown and sticky?**

The first time you heard this you were probably thinking of all the brown, sticky and smelly things in the world! But here comes the answer:

> **A stick!**

Surprise! It's not rude at all, and now you're thinking about how you've been tricked by two meanings of the word 'sticky'. It's a very clever joke.

So let's try something easier: a pun. Puns are great fun for kids because the sillier they are, the better! Here's how it works. Start with a great word: **humbug**. In Britain, a humbug is a type of hard, minty sweet or candy (yummy). But what does humbug *sound* like? It sounds like a joke!

> **What do you call an insect that doesn't know the words?**
> A humbug!

That's just the start. Find humbug rhymes – even if they're not real words – and you can make lots more jokes!

How? Just go through the alphabet letter by letter, changing the first sound (ignore the vowels: a, e, i, o & u).
· Don't forget that some sounds are made up of more than one letter, like cr-, ch- and th-.
· If you're feeling adventurous, you can use 'nearly' rhymes, too. As long as the word sounds similar, it's good!

Let's try it out with **h**umbug:

b➤   **b**umbug. Oops, what a way to start: I made a rude word! I won't use that one or I'll be in trouble!

c➤   **c**omebug. That's good! Let me think...

> **What do you call an obedient insect?**
> A comebug!

Not bad, but I bet you can do better! What about chumbug, or crumbug? Dumbug? It's your turn!

How did you get on? Have you invented a brand new bug joke?

Great! Now every awesome joke needs a fantastic illustration, just like the ones in this book by super-clever Indrek. He's really thought about the jokes, and added lots of extra detail to make them even funnier.

So now you can do the same. Use the page opposite to tell and draw your bug joke, and don't forget to make that picture really funny!

If you'd like a bigger sheet to draw on, you can download one to print out at *matwaugh.co.uk/wall*

Happy? Ask a grown-up to take a picture and send it to jokes@matwaugh.co.uk – I'll put all the best ones on the **Wall Of Awesome Jokes** on my website.

Happy bug hunting!

Parents: see the website for full terms and conditions.

My Awesome Joke!

Question:

Answer:

My illustration:

My first name: _____ Age: _____

Home town and country: _____

MORE AWESOME JOKES EVERY 8 YEAR OLD SHOULD KNOW!

Phew, we're done!

Reviews of joke books are almost as funny as the books themselves.

You're not funny!
These jokes are too old!
These jokes are for babies!
These jokes are too rude!

I get all of those and I don't mind: it just shows that everyone is different! But if you have something nice to say about this book, or you're just really funny – then please pop over to Amazon with your parent and write something about this book so others know what to expect.

As long as you found something to laugh about, I'm happy too!

About Mat Waugh

In the first book, I told you about my batty aunt. Here are some new things about me.

I have big crow's feet. I know what you're thinking – how do I buy my shoes? But crow's feet are those wrinkles that grown-ups get next to their eyes.

Some people get crow's feet because they need glasses but don't wear them enough (true).

Some people get them because their skin doesn't have enough oil, called sebum. I only included this fact because then I can write the word *see-bum*. (What?! That's how you say it!).

But I get crow's feet because I spend a lot of time squinting at my three children, trying to give them Paddington hard stares. They ignore me.

I've jumped out of a plane, done bungee jumps and tried wreck diving. I even met Mrs Waugh at a theme park. But last week I got dizzy on the trampoline. The lesson? **Never get old, children!**

I still can't do handstands. I'm practising.

I produce enough dribble each day to fill a water bottle, and enough each year to fill the bath.*

My favourite sounds are birdsong, tapping keys, and windmills.

When I was 19 I had a ticket for a flight with some friends, but there wasn't enough space. The airline put us on a tiny plane instead and I sat in the co-pilot's seat. While my friends were sleeping in the back, the pilot let me have a go at flying the plane.

I've taken a photo of my daughters every single Sunday since they were born. I'm very proud of this, as I'm not very good at homework. In nearly every photo, they're pulling a silly face at me.

Finally, I love getting emails (but ask your parents first!). You can reach me here: mail@matwaugh.co.uk

* So do you!

Three more to try!

Cheeky Charlie series
Meet Harriet and her small, stinky brother. Together, they're trouble. Fabulously funny stories that will keep you snorting way past bedtime.

Fantastic Wordsearches
Wordsearch with a difference: themed, crossword clues and hidden words await!

The Fun Factor
When the fun starts vanishing from Thora's village, she's the only one to notice. Frosty the headmaster is definitely up to no good, but what about Dad's new girlfriend? A mystery adventure story for gadget-loving kids aged 8+.

Available from Amazon and local bookshops.

Be the first to know about new stuff! Sign up for my emails at matwaugh.co.uk

Made in the USA
Middletown, DE
19 December 2022

19614177R00061